RENAULT 4

MARK BRADBURY

AMBERLEY

First published 2022

Amberley Publishing
The Hill, Stroud,
Gloucestershire, GL5 4EP

www.amberley-books.com

ISBN: 978 1 3981 1335 0 (print)
ISBN: 978 1 3981 1336 7 (ebook)

British Library Cataloguing in Publication Data.
A catalogue record for this book is available from the British Library.

Typeset in 10pt on 13pt Celeste.
Typesetting by SJmagic DESIGN SERVICES, India.
Printed in the UK.

Contents

Acknowledgements

Firstly, I am extremely grateful to motoring journalist and author Malcolm Bobbitt for suggesting to Amberley Publishing that I might be a suitable author for a Renault 4 book. Malcolm's tireless help, suggestions and proofreading have helped to make this project so very enjoyable.

Thanks are extended to the Renault UK Press Office, in particular Yasmin Rhodes and her colleagues, for accessing the Renault Classic archives in Paris on my behalf and allowing me to use their images in this book. I am also indebted to renowned Renault historian Hector Mackenzie-Wintle and Renault Classic Car Club chairman Brian Whiteside, for their extensive marque knowledge and for fact-checking the completed draft.

I must also thank Tony Vos (editor of classic Renault magazine losangemagazine.com) for kindly allowing me to use his photographs, and for checking over the text prior to publication. I'm also much obliged to Stephen Laing for his comments on the draft. Other images were supplied by Andrew Minney, Nina Smith, Geraldine de Comtes, Erich Karsholt, Julien Miss and, with the shots of his rather special and very early R4, Mikaël Peyre.

My long-suffering wife, Jill, must also be mentioned here. As a professional photographer, Jill's help was invaluable not only for helping me to take some of the shots but for choosing the best images for the book. She has also put up with months of endless chatter about all things Renault 4.

Every attempt has been made to seek permission for copyright material used in this book. However, if we have inadvertently used copyright material without permission or acknowledgement we apologise and will make the necessary correction at the first opportunity.

Introduction

Just occasionally a car comes along which, for whatever reason, seems to resonate with people and forms an important part of the social fabric; at risk of being accused of using a somewhat well-worn cliché, it becomes a legend in its own lifetime.

It can be subjective but few would argue that the original Mini and the Morris Minor – both courtesy of Sir Alec Issigonis – would be definite candidates. The equally special and

A beautifully restored and very early example of the basic model Renault R4. This is the twenty-ninth built and dates from mid-1961. With various additional brackets on the rear suspension, it was more than likely to have been used by Renault for testing. The base R4 is virtually indistinguishable from the R3; it proudly displays the blanked-in rear quarter, simple tubular bumpers and pressed metal grille but also the flat bonnet without the centre ribbing of all later models. (Peyre)

well-loved Citroën 2CV and Volkswagen Beetle were even earlier members of the club; and one certainly shouldn't forget the Fiat 500 and Nuova.

Another contender might be the Ford Model T. As the second best-selling, basically unchanged, car in the world (after the Volkswagen Beetle), it is generally regarded as the first affordable car that finally made inexpensive motoring available to virtually everyone, and paved the way for many other manufacturers to adopt mass production techniques – not least the manufacturer behind the subject of this publication. While there can be no doubt that Henry's masterpiece is an important car, the passage of time since it was commonplace on our roads means it is probably not viewed with quite the same fondness as those already mentioned.

Apart from minor facelifts and mechanical improvements, the vehicle in question must be substantially unchanged throughout its production period, and not one which has sold spectacularly well as a specific make and model across half a dozen or more series or marks.

There is another, often overlooked, candidate for this rather special band of automotive greats, and that's the Renault 4. Conceived out of necessity in the 1950s and born in 1961, the Gallic utilitarian runabout remained in production pretty well unchanged for just over thirty years.

Having a grey plastic grille and matching bumpers, bumperettes and body protectors, this is a post-1978 1108 cc GTL model. It's one of the earlier GTLs though with the air intake exposed below the grille and the dash-top-mounted rear-view mirror. The Renault 4 remained basically unchanged throughout its thirty-year production. (Vos)

The Renault 4 was very successful as a commercial vehicle and was officially called the F4, or Fourgonnette. This one is the long-wheelbase version (with several inches being added to the wheelbase) known as the F6 with a 9 cwt load capacity instead of 7. The numbering scheme is deliberate and corresponds to the car's taxable horsepower rating. (Renault)

The Renault was popular too, with more than eight million built or assembled, and sold, across many of the world's countries. It is not only the third best-selling car ever, and top of the list in France, but it helped to save the French car manufacturer from financial collapse while managing to achieve that very hard-won position in the lasting affections of both owners and occupants alike. It is this little car, loved by millions over three generations, that this book aims to discuss, describe, celebrate and propose as the French people's car – a full sixty years in the making!

Renault – A Brief History

The Renault story began in France as early as 1898 when a young Louis Renault started out on his engineering odyssey. One of three brothers and the fourth of six children, Louis was born on 12 February 1877 into the well-off Parisian family of Alfred and Berthe Renault. Fascinated by mechanics and engines, he took over his parent's garden shed at the bottom of the family garden in Boulogne-Billancourt, then a relatively unknown and fairly rural area of Paris, and built his first car.

This was still the beginning of the development of the motor car as we recognise it today; indeed, it was only a couple of years after the emancipation of the motorist when they could drive at a heady 12 mph instead of 4, and without a man walking a few yards in front carrying a red flag. This freedom remains a point of celebration to this very day

Louis Renault 1877–1944. (Renault)

with the annual London to Brighton Veteran Car Run for motorised vehicles manufactured prior to 1905, which incidentally, is not only the world's longest-running motoring event, but is also patronised by at least a dozen early and rather lovely Renaults to form one of the larger groups of a specific marque.

Before embarking on his motor manufacturing career, Louis had spent many long hours in his bedroom at home devouring anything relating to practical engineering and shirking the more academic side of his education. Louis filed a patent for a type of steam boiler but additionally nurtured a growing interest in the increasingly popular internal combustion engine and it was this, coupled with a spell of service in the infantry where he was able to dabble in yet more mechanical matters, which led him to acquire a De Dion tricycle which would form the basis of his first car.

Louis Renault's first car – the prototype – was built in 1898 and used the De Dion engine with a light, tubular steel frame and a simple, two-seater body. With the addition of four cycle wheels with pneumatic tyres, its suspension comprised full-elliptic leaf springs at the front and rear. One feature which was unusual at that time and considered quite innovative was the use of drive shafts with an early type of universal joint instead of the traditional belts or chains. The prototype had several novel features and Louis gave onlookers an impromptu demonstration of its abilities by driving up the steep Rue Lepic in Montmartre. Enthralled by its driving simplicity and lightness, some of his audience placed their orders on the spot. At this point Renault had barely reached the age of twenty-one but the seeds of one of the giants of the automobile world were well and truly sown.

It's Christmas 1898 and Louis Renault's prototype Voiturette is finished. Impressed by how easy it was to drive, several of his friends wanted their own. With the success of the prototype, the following year Renault Frères started producing motor cars. This picture shows a tentative Louis Renault behind the wheel of a very early version. (Renault)

A Company is Formed

As a result of the unexpected interest Louis received in the prototype, in early 1899 he and his two brothers, Marcel and Fernand, invested 60,000 francs to form Renault Frères. With its registered office at 10 Avenue du Cours, Boulogne-Billancourt, an announcement was made in the local press to the effect that their objective was to manufacture motor cars.

The entrance to the Renault Frères workshops and offices at Rue du Point du Jour, Boulogne-Billancourt in 1905. Most Renaults of the era, like the Type N and AG pictured here, have the then trademark sloping engine cover. In order to retain the so-called 'coal scuttle' bonnet the coolant radiator was mounted at the back of the engine with flywheel-mounted fan blades ensuring a cooling breeze over the core was ever present. Cautious as ever, Louis protected the arrangement with patents. (Renault)

The Voiturette had many modern features, including a front-mounted engine, a driveshaft and a direct-drive gearbox patented by Louis Renault. The production Type A depicted here was unveiled in June 1899. Just a couple of months later, Louis and his brother Marcel drove a similar model to second place in the Amateur Drivers' Cup event from Paris to Trouville. This driver is fully attired for the trip ahead while a curious shopkeeper is wondering what this newfangled thing might be. (Renault)

The brothers split the work depending on their individual talents: Louis was nominated Chief Engineer, Marcel took on the role of Managing Director and the post of Accountant fell to Fernand. Using the prototype car as a basis and having employed some additional workforce, Renault Frères was in business and they developed their first production model, the Renault Type A, or Voiturette.

Things started rather cautiously with a two-year plan being devised, proposing the building of thirty cars. This was a reasonable target given that the demand for motorised vehicles at the start of the 1900s was minimal, and stemmed from the most wealthy. By the summer of 1899 however (and after just six months), the new company had built sixty Type As and were busy designing the follow-on model, the Type B.

Early Success

Before the first year of trading had been completed and following a very successful Paris Salon showing of a production car in June 1899, Renault had nearly eighty orders for their Types A and B. While Louis was fiercely protective of his innovations, he also realised that the company's cars had to be simple to build and straightforward to drive.

During the very early years of Renault, the brothers began to take an active part in motor sport and entered their Voiturettes in many great road races of the time with Louis and Marcel taking the top two podium positions in the Paris–Trouville race in August 1899. They went on to further competition successes, the publicity securing them sales of some 200 cars.

Increasing numbers of orders meant enlarging the size of the factory and employing a greater number of workers and, by 1903, Renault's workforce had grown to more than 600 employees building nearly 3,000 vehicles. Apart from swelling the order books, racing also led to technical improvements and Renault soon designed its first engine, culminating in the 1902 Paris–Vienna race-winning 30 bhp, four–cylinder, 3.8 litre Type K. A development of this motor found its way into a 14/20 Landaulette purchased in 1906 by HM King Edward VII and, with various modern accoutrements such as heating for both passengers and chauffeur, more reliable cooling and lubrication systems, and not least the royal endorsement, Renault motor cars found favour with other notable motorists of the time.

Sadly, despite Renault's success this was a difficult time for Louis; Marcel was killed in 1903 while competing in his Renault in the Paris–Madrid race, and Fernand died in 1909 following an illness. Not wishing to lose control of the company, Louis managed to buy his late brothers' shares and became sole owner of the company which had now become La Société Louis Renault. By 1913, Renault was producing around 20 per cent of all French cars.

With the advent of the First World War there was a switch to munitions with tank production being Renault's mainstay, in addition to light arms. Just as the conflict was coming to an end in 1918 the then forty-year-old Louis married Christiane Boullaire, nineteen years his junior. The couple had a son, Jean-Louis, and they lived in the rather grand Chateau Herqueville on the banks of the Seine in Paris. Following the Armistice, Renault had further competition successes including wins at Le Mans and it was also the first manufacturer to average more than a hundred miles an hour for twelve hours on the Montlhéry banked circuit. In 1922 the name of the firm was changed again, becoming Société Anonyme des Usines Renault (SAUR).

A Different Focus

Meeting the demand for mass motoring during the interwar years was not lost on Louis Renault, who understood the future lay in building small- and medium-sized cars. Accordingly, he established factories on the banks of the Seine which allowed for easy deliveries of finished vehicles. The business flourished and in 1938 Renault produced its first unitary-constructed model, the Juvaquatre. It was not particularly new mechanically and it was criticised for resembling Germany's Opel Kadett, but the new car nevertheless helped address the need for fuel-economic cars in France, which within a few years would be hugely intensified.

Despite the success of the company, the end of the 1930s signalled a slow decline for Louis Renault. Not only was his health declining, but he had won himself few friends, both personally and politically. Visiting the 1938 Berlin Motor Show he was reportedly impressed by the prototype KdF-Wagen, or what would ultimately become the Volkswagen Beetle. The evidence is that seeing the German 'people's car' influenced him to follow the growing trend and design a rear-engined car for himself. While he was in the German capital, a meeting with Adolf Hitler had been arranged by the French ambassador François Poncet. Very little is known of the dialogue between the Nazi leader and Renault, but the very act of the discussion led to much ill-feeling not only with the French press but also with the factory workers at Boulogne-Billancourt.

Barely eighteen months later with the onset of war, everything was set to change. Renault as a company had prospered while Louis Renault had risen to become one of Europe's wealthiest industrialists and, then as elsewhere in Europe, car production gave way to essential war work.

The subsequent Nazi occupation of France led to the seizure of the Renault factory and it began building vehicles for the German war machine. Louis Renault considered that he had little choice other than to capitulate but, following the liberation of Paris, he was accused by his left-wing enemies of collaboration and, as a frail, sixty-seven-year-old, he was taken to the prison at Fresnes allegedly for his own protection. After being moved to the Ville-Evrard psychiatric hospital and then to Saint-Jean-de-Dieu private nursing home, Louis Renault died on 24 October 1944 and was buried at the family's chateau. France had lost one of its most talented engineers and one of the true fathers of the modern motor car.

Rising from the Ashes

As peace came to France, what was left of the Renault company took stock. It was estimated that more than half of the buildings and machinery had been lost, along with virtually all the designs and files of information. In order to help rebuild war-torn France, employment, motor vehicles and foreign trade would be needed. Renault had been a solid provider of this

Pierre Lefaucheux 1898–1955. (Renault)

before the hostilities but now needed serious help, so in 1946 President Charles de Gaulle nationalised Renault to become Régie Nationale des Usines Renault, and appointed Pierre Lefaucheux as President. It is convenient to note here that the company is affectionately referred to by Renault aficionados as Régie Renault or usually just plain Régie.

Born on 30 June 1898 at Triel-sur-Seine, Pierre Lefaucheux was the second of four children of Pierre André Lefaucheux and Madeleine Dulac. Following his voluntary service in the First World War and his exemplary military record, he was awarded the Croix de Guerre, a decoration given for acts of heroism involving combat with the enemy. During the Second World War, Lefaucheux had been arrested by the Gestapo and rescued by Marie-Hélène Postel-Vinay, whom he subsequently married. They were both members of the French Resistance and Marie-Hélène was actively involved in the liberation of Paris, later becoming a prominent political figure in the United Nations.

It was the view of Pierre Lefaucheux that building affordable cars was the route to Renault's survival, and that the rear-engined concept inspired by Louis during the war would ensure the company's future. With the pre-war large Renaults a very distant memory, the resulting model – to be called the 4CV – was set to appeal to those wanting a small and economic car. It was also anticipated that with worldwide exports, France might be able to earn the foreign exchange it so sorely needed.

The 4CV was first in a line of rear-engined Renaults which included the very successful Dauphine of 1956, as well as the shapely Floride and Caravelle of a couple of years later. The Dauphine was a bigger car than the 4CV and, fitted with a similar engine but in 845cc form, it sold well in both Europe and North America where it briefly overtook the Volkswagen Beetle. It would also share some of the competition glory enjoyed by the 4CV with an outright win in the 1958 Monte Carlo Rally at the hands of Guy Monraisse and Jacques Feret.

Produced from 1956 to 1967 and bigger than the 4CV, the Dauphine was rear-engined but used the more powerful 845 cc Billancourt engine. This rather soiled Dauphine has presumably stopped to get an Esso Tiger in its tank. The slogan was created in 1959 by Chicagoan Emery Smith but the big cat had been a mascot for Esso in Norway around half a century before, so can't help us date this image. The split rims and frontal treatment indicate it's an early car; it also looks like notes are being taken. Details of fuel consumption perhaps? (Renault)

The Frégate was a big front-engined, rear-wheel drive car with a 2-litre engine dramatically upscaled from the 4CV unit. With rushed development (it was intended to be rear-engined like its smaller sibling) and having gained a reputation for being unreliable, it was further blighted when company boss Pierre Lefaucheux suffered a fatal accident in one. On a happier note, this idyllic photo is set in one of Renault's favourite photography locations, Honfleur in northern France. (Renault)

Pierre Dreyfus 1907–94. (Renault)

Lefaucheux was aware of the capacity issues that the aging Boulogne-Billancourt plant was suffering and in 1948 he went on a search for a site to build a new factory. He found a suitable area on the banks of the Seine around 25 miles west of Paris with excellent road, rail and river links and work soon started on his personal project, the Flins factory.

Flins was very modern and efficient, the showcase of Renault, and from 1951 began manufacturing the relatively large front-engined Frégate model.

On 11 February 1955, Lefaucheux was scheduled to give a presentation to a Catholic student club in Strasbourg about the post-war transformation of the Régie. He was a keen driver and despite the wintry weather decided to travel by car rather than by train, having declared it to be quicker. Just outside Saint-Dizier, his car spun on black ice and rolled over. In a bizarre and very unlucky quirk of fate, the bag he'd left on the back seat of his Renault Frégate struck him on the nape of the neck and he was killed instantly. Highly respected by both workforce and management alike, both the Flins plant and a Paris boulevard were named after Pierre Lefaucheux, and a memorial stone was erected near the site of the accident. Lefaucheux was succeeded by the then Renault vice-president, Pierre Dreyfus.

At forty-eight years old, Dreyfus was totally different from his predecessor in both stature and personality but was utterly devoted to the future of the Renault empire. For various reasons, Dreyfus didn't consider himself to be the most suitable candidate and he took some convincing to take on the role. He finally agreed but told the Renault Board he only planned to stay in the job for a maximum of two years, and he wouldn't work past 6 p.m. because of various domestic commitments. He was a leader of exceptional ability and soon started to organise things his way. He told his board of eleven top executives that he didn't know much about cars but published a constantly updated, five-year plan and, with exports a national necessity, he announced an annual target for Renault to send at least half of the total production overseas, sending shockwaves around the business.

Dreyfus immediately set about getting the new Dauphine into production at Flins, and it became very successful at home and abroad. He knew though that his long-term plans to take Renault into the next decade wouldn't come to fruition without replacing the by now much-loved 4CV. The typical family would need practical, functional and economic transport, so he instructed his team to build an inexpensive car that would 'carry a lot of things', and hence the Renault 4 – his first car – was conceived.

Despite those initial uncertainties about his suitability for the top job and the self-imposed conditions, Dreyfus stayed for no less than twenty years and he would often work until very late in the evenings. There is absolutely no doubt that much of the success of Renault in the post-war period can be attributed to him. He eventually retired from the company in 1975 and died on Christmas Day 1994.

Modern Times

With a few other notable successes into the 1960s and beyond, including the 16, the 5 and the very successful and brilliantly marketed Clio, Renault's growth as a car manufacturer was assured. Following its early competition success, Renault returned to sport with a vengeance, bringing the turbocharger to Formula 1 in 1977 and its own grand prix team eight years later. After a twenty-year spell in the F1, Renault engines had won nearly one hundred grand prix and four world drivers' championships, including those for Britain's Nigel Mansell and Damon Hill. The company's cars also won the Le Mans 24 Hours Grand Prix d'Endurance, six Monte Carlo Rallies and countless other minor events.

Today, the Renault Group comprises five brands – Renault, Dacia, Lada, Alpine and Mobilize – in more than 130 countries. It remains partly owned by the French state but more than half is now in public ownership. With just over 170,000 employees and a net income of some eight billion euros, it is the ninth largest motor manufacturer in the world. Renault's headquarters remain not very far from where it all started at Boulogne-Billancourt.

The garden shed where Louis Renault's engineering work began has been painstakingly preserved by the factory and is in its original position not far from the main offices. In the world of Renault, 'Billancourt' will forever be associated with the marque.

Louis Renault's very early development work began in his parent's garden shed in Boulogne-Billancourt, in what would become the grounds of the first Renault factory. The shed – depicted here in an early shot – has been carefully preserved and forever reminds employees and visitors alike of the origins and history of the company. (Renault)

2

Post-war Success – The 4CV

During the occupation of France, Louis Renault had been secretly working on a new small rear-engined car which he felt would help mobilise the French nation after the war. With a small team of trusted fellow engineers, they managed to build a few rough prototypes and a couple of development engines. Shrouded in secrecy, they took the cars out on very careful and secluded test drives. It was reported that they performed very well and managed to maintain an easy 50 mph with four people on board. While the concept was no doubt inspired by Louis Renault, his health was by this time very compromised and most of the development work was completed by his loyal colleagues, led by Fernand Picard and Charles Edmond Serre.

There is no denying that the proposed design bore more than just a passing resemblance to the German car that Louis Renault had seen in Berlin – the prototype Volkswagen Beetle. This leads to a commonly held misconception that Ferdinand Porsche had been involved in the creation of the 4CV but, in reality, the similarity of the overall shape of the body with its rear engine layout simply reflects the styling and engineering trends of the time. Given the enforced German war work Renault had to endure, it is very unlikely he would have allowed anyone else to have had a major say in the new car.

La Motte de Beurre

With the death of Louis Renault in 1944 and the factory in total disarray, his successor, Pierre Lefaucheux, decided that the two-door prototype car devised and developed during hostilities would be the company's salvation. Within just a couple of years he had managed to resurrect most of the work along with a couple of prototypes and, with further development, launched the Renault 4CV in September 1946. One significant change Lefaucheux made was to insist on the fitting of four-doors to satisfy customer demand and moreover, being a big man, he would have had difficulty squeezing himself into the rear seats. The car made its press debut that September and its public appearance a few weeks later but, with post-war shortages, it was available in one colour

With its rear-engine cooling louvres and rounded body, it's easy to see why people think the 4CV – better known as the 750 in Britain – *may* have been copied from the German rival. The chrome cap beneath the rear window is not for petrol but coolant, and causes no end of trouble if mixed up. The car nearest the camera is a fairly early one, evident from the split (or 'detachable') rim roadwheels. (Author)

only, the sand yellow ex-Africa Korps paint being a throwback to Renault's war work. Given the hue and the car's rounded shape, it was affectionally referred to as *La motte de beurre*, or the butter pat.

The 4CV, with its rear-positioned wet-liner and alloy-headed 760 cc engine mated to a three-speed gearbox, was judged by the media as being particularly advanced for its time. The drivetrain layout with the final drive located in front of the power unit added to the 4CV's compactness while all-round independent suspension, hydraulic brakes, and rack and pinion steering ensured it was a pleasure to drive.

Apart from its impressive technical specification, the car had some interesting design touches. With 'suicide' front doors hinged from the B-post using the same pivot points as the rears, a neat solution coupled with a worthwhile cost saving was introduced. The catch-cum-handle for the front luggage compartment doubled up as an attractively slender chrome strip along the centre of the panel. With the engine tucked away behind the rear seat, there was clearly a need for an air intake, which was addressed by the delicate-looking bright metal grilles, or gills, in the leading edges of the rear wheel arches. A delightfully short and precise gear lever appealed to enthusiastic motorists, and the lights and horn were operated via a steering wheel mounted stalk – an arrangement virtually unheard of at the time.

One feature which did cause a few problems was the position of the radiator cap. The shiny cap mounted centrally below the rear window was more prominent than the petrol filler, which resided under the engine compartment lid, and occasionally there were reports of careless garage attendants getting an unexpected facial sauna when all they really meant to do was uncork the fuel tank. It is worth noting that in Britain the 4CV was more usually referred to as the Renault 760, or later with the engine capacity change, the Renault 750.

Sales Success

Production problems and industrial disputes at the Boulogne-Billancourt factory meant buyers had to wait until 1947 before taking delivery of their new Renaults. Lefaucheux was very aware of the importance of a proper launch and made the car available in 300 French towns with all the pomp and ceremony that could be mustered in times of great austerity. Buyers rushed to place their orders with the result that delivery dates doubled from one to two years. It was not unusual for early purchasers, having taken delivery of their cars, to immediately sell them at a much higher price, thus creating a 'black market'. Much to Renault's annoyance, some of those early purchasers chose to sell on their cars to these eager potential owners, patiently waiting in the queue, and made a decent profit.

By early 1949, 300 cars a day were being produced to realise Pierre Lefaucheux's strategy of the 4CV revitalising the company. Twelve months later the daily total rose to 400 and, that same year, the 100,000th 4CV rolled off the production line making it at the time France's best-selling car. In April 1954, half a million had been constructed and, by the end of its production seven years later, the figure surpassed one million – the first French car to do so.

Competition Success

The 4CV's alloy head engine soon proved itself to be very robust and capable of being tuned to produce greater performance and, with bigger valves, multiple choke carburettors

A very late 4CV Sport or model 1063. Seen here at rest alongside the Seine on a lovely summer's day, they were usually in full flight at the hands of an amateur rally or racing driver. Unlike the hot-hatches of later years, there were no obvious signs of its performance potential and, being a very late version, it is devoid of its split rims although it retains the delicate cooling vents, or gills, in the rear arches. (Renault)

and big-bore exhaust, the amount of power could be doubled. Additional potency is of no benefit, however, if the car doesn't handle safely. Thankfully, the car was gifted with a relatively low centre of gravity along with compliant springing, precise steering and, with wheels positioned at each corner, the Renault was a delight to drive in a spirited fashion on twisty roads.

The Renault proved itself to be the machine that keen motorists had been waiting for and quickly became considered an accomplished competition car. In July 1948, three 4CVs tackled the 1,125 miles of the Circuit of the Alps and finished inside the fixed time limits. A couple of months later they took the top five places in their class in a race up Mont Ventoux, with one driver averaging almost 40 mph. It was this kind of competition success that led to the establishment of a team of Renault works drivers.

The 4CV excelled in the Monte-Carlo Rally with Louis Rosier winning the 750 to 1100 cc class in 1949, and, two years later when the engine size dropped to 747 cc, Rosier, Lecat and Kreisel took the top three places in the under 750 cc category. In 1951 the Régie entered a team comprising five French racing blue 4CVs in the Le Mans 24 Hours endurance race. Three cars finished with François Landon and André Briat driving number 50 claiming a class win.

In acknowledging the 4CV's sporting ability, Renault brought out its own road-going version of the works car in 1952. The Sports version was given a modified engine with a dual-choke carburettor producing around 42 bhp plus an option of a five-speed, non-synchromesh gearbox. Demand for the limited production-run special was brisk, it being particularly popular with the rally fraternity.

The Need for a New Small Car

The Renault 4CV had quickly won acclaim for its fine build quality and handling. It won many friends in France and beyond, and not least Britain, where it was assembled at the company's Acton factory in London. Contemporary British road test features reveal the car made an interesting change from the average homespun models. In addition to Acton, the 4CV was built in six other countries and, with a final tally in 1961 of 1,105,543 cars, the model was (and remains) a truly great design and thus proved itself as the car that put Renault back on its feet.

Despite – or perhaps because of – the amazing success of the 4CV, Lefaucheux's successor Pierre Dreyfus knew the car was dated and, to ensure continued growth of the company, it simply had to be replaced. With its less than commodious luggage space, rear-mounted engine and very rounded styling still displaying the pronounced front and rear wings, something fresh and totally different was needed. After more than a decade of peace, and with a population brimming with hope and opportunities both in France and abroad, Dreyfus decided that a true multi-role car was required. It still had to be inexpensive to build and buy as well as being functional but now it needed to have more interior space and appeal to country and city dwellers alike.

Au revoir 4CV et bonjour Renault 4!

A 1958 750 captured very recently and in fine condition. Fitted with a 747 cc version of the Billancourt engine which would eventually find a home in its successor, the Renault 4 – albeit rotating in the other direction to aid the use of the starting handle. Beautifully built and finished off, the chrome bonnet centre strip doubles as the front compartment catch, and the engine cooling gills are visible just in front of the rear wheels. (Author)

3

Design and Development of the Renault 4

With his thoughts firmly focused on the need for a totally different car, in early 1956 Pierre Dreyfus launched Project 112, the internal Renault code for the car that would ultimately become the Renault 4.

After the war, the Citroën 2CV had been aimed towards the farming community and their transportation requirements but it quickly became a classless car that was equally at home in the big cities. Times were changing and Dreyfus became convinced that what was wanted

One of the first R4 running prototypes. The overall shape bears some resemblance to the final product but lacks a certain finesse. The three-stud wheels are evident although they look smaller with a rather slab-sided wheel-arch area. The basic (early) grille shape however does look to be largely in place. (Renault)

was a relatively inexpensive, go-anywhere, put-anything-in-it vehicle to compete with, but improve upon, the 2CV. It had to address the needs of modern society and, with remarkably progressive thinking, he knew it needn't be restricted to France. Across Europe people were leaving the countryside in droves as modernity and the desire for urban life swept through the post-war landscape. Farming was very important to most countries including France (and would remain so) but suburbs would become the new place, part rural and part urban. It was here where Dreyfus saw the need for a vehicle that could easily cope with a bit of everything; the time when city cars would be different from country cars was over.

A Changing Population

As the 1950s gathered pace, the population prospered and the suburban areas grew. With the inevitable greater wealth from better jobs in a thriving post-war economy came

Jumping ahead to the mid-1960s, the driver of this R4L is taking a well-earned rest in the picturesque harbour town of Honfleur – maybe she's waiting for someone to sail in? In northern France's Normandy region, Honfleur is on the estuary where the Seine meets the English Channel and over the centuries has attracted artists including Claude Monet. It has proven a popular location for factory photography. (Renault)

You can't usually drive a car onto the fairway – unless it's a photo shoot and probably not even a real golf course anyway. This is the open-topped and doorless version of the 4 called the Plein Air, or 'Outdoors', and popular in warmer climes as beachfront transport perhaps. Built from 1968 using standard R4s by Renault group company Sinpar, around 500 were produced until the more rugged Rodeo – also a soft-top – superseded it in the early 1970s. (Renault)

more private motor vehicles. Many women had stayed on in their work after the war and dual-income households were no longer unusual. As working conditions improved, companies provided perks such as regular leisure time in the form of weekends and paid annual holidays. Trips away, possibly to the coast or the countryside, beckoned and there was no better way to do it than in one's own motor car.

The R4 was adept – by design – at carrying people and their chattels along rough and bumpy roads including sandy beaches. This group are intent on spending serious quality time at the seaside and with shelter, a seat and a cool box, they seem to be relatively well prepared. The sunroof was doubtless very welcome en route but by the expression on the face of the chap in the shorts, he's suddenly realised he forgot to pack the picnic. (Renault)

With various business and leisure requirements involving longer trips at the higher speeds permitted by the newly emerging autoroute system, the modern motor vehicle would need better performance. A car wouldn't just be for church on Sunday and market on Monday; it would need to be capable of carrying all sorts of loads over ever greater distances, and often much more quickly than before.

The car was no longer a plaything for the wealthy; it was becoming an essential part of social life and the family unit. With more and more households able to venture into the world of motoring, the issuing of licences flourished. The car now belonged to the whole family; they all took an interest in what to buy, and shrewd manufacturers and dealerships cashed in. The new Renault had to appeal to everyone; it was the weekday workhorse; the weekend runabout; holiday transport for the whole family. Dreyfus and his team knew this and were able to respond.

Initial Concept

Following on from the need for a 'go anywhere' vehicle, Dreyfus came up with the notion of the 'blue jeans car'. Denim clothing could be worn by anyone to do just about anything,

No matter how good the artist's impressions and drawings might be, a 3D version is hard to beat to really assess a proposed design. Here a quarter-scale clay model is being sculpted and, from the various design cues such as the rear door shape and grille outline, it looks like it's very close to the final car. (Renault)

Artist's impressions are always important and here's a relatively late rendering of the design in the form of a coloured drawing. The grille shape is not quite right though, and a 'Renault' script that didn't get through to the final version is also evident on the front wing. (Minney)

anywhere – it was classless and affordable. Just like a pair of Levis, he had the notion that the new car should also be 'versatile enough to go anywhere, do anything and be convenient for all occasions'. He added, 'It should be inexpensive with a worldwide calling which could match the changes in society that were being observed as the 1960s approached.' With his ideas now firmly established, his design team led by Fernand Picard went ahead with project 112. The new car also had to have a list price limited to 350,000 francs, 'and not a centime more', and so informally the design team referred to it as the 350.

A roomy interior was something Dreyfus requested. 'Give me space!' he told his team, 'I want a holdall on wheels – a travelling bag that can go anywhere without feeling self-conscious. It must be as tough as a rhino and cost a lot less to run. People will go to church in it, will go camping, will commute to the office, will make it a livestock carrier, a shop, a wedding car, a passion wagon...'. At that time cars were simply an engine usually driving the rear wheels, seats and a boot meaning internal space was compromised by the transmission and rear axle or, in the case of Renault's very own 4CV, the power unit itself.

The suspension could also intrude and waste valuable room; the 2CV had overcome some of these shortcomings with a very compact design of suspension and front-wheel drive, but Dreyfus was sure there was much more that could be done.

It was inevitable that the rival at Citroën would feature very highly in the thoughts of Pierre Dreyfus. The Deux Chevaux represented his main competition and, with the benefit of it being launched at least ten years before, Dreyfus was able to critique it and he was certain, make something better. It has been suggested that Renault copied from their opposite number but this is both untrue and unfair; indeed, Dreyfus had a lot of respect for his competitors. All manufacturers, not just those making cars, look at similar items on the market and learn from them. This is not copying or plagiarism but it's part of the

This couple are clearly delighted with the luggage they've managed to cram into their new R4L. The car had its Danish premiere at the Danish Motor Show in the Forum in Copenhagen in March 1962, and these two young actors were tasked by the Danish importers to perform a short play based around a picnic scene to extol the virtues of the new car. It was reported to be a 'sensation'. (Karsholt)

process of product design, development and advancement – one only needs to examine the range of Superminis and Sports Utility Vehicles on the market today and this becomes abundantly clear.

Suspension

Providing the extra space that Dreyfus craved led to the decision to adopt front-wheel drive. He had never been a fan of *traction avant* but reasoned for the new model it was an absolute necessity. Apart from improved drivability, keeping the engine and transmission forward of

Designed to let potential buyers view the inner parts of the car, this motor show display yields the mechanical layout and passenger accommodation very effectively. The front and rear torsion bar suspension is also revealed, and what might not be obvious from this static view is the wheelbase difference and that the rig is actually articulated; in a carefully choreographed operation the three parts move apart and back together using cables and a multitude of electric motors. Spot the contemporaries: a Dauphine to one side and a Citroën DS nestling in the background. (Renault)

the passenger compartment would create a large flat floor for both passengers and luggage, and would be further enhanced by the adoption of a space-saving suspension design. The suspension was a challenge; it not only had to intrude only a minimal amount into the passenger compartment – if at all – but it had to provide a large amount of travel to cope with the less than smooth rural French roads, plus endow the car with a well-damped ride and handling for higher-speed motorway use. They were not after a sports car; it just had to cope with the rigours of varying road surfaces and loads.

After exploring various systems, the final layout was determined. With double wishbones and an anti-roll bar at the front, twin trailing arms at the rear, torsion bar springs front and back coupled with rack and pinion steering, it was certainly modern. Two longitudinal torsion bars from the lower wishbones back to the chassis dealt with the front, while a pair of transverse, parallel torsion bars were fitted at the rear. With this set-up, fully independent suspension had been achieved and all of the performance and intrusion requirements had been met. With one rear torsion bar tucked behind the other, the wheelbase on the right-hand side of the car ended up a couple of inches longer than the left. The design team reasoned that in a utilitarian car any minor compromise in handling could be tolerated, if not just simply accepted and, after many thousands of kilometres of testing, they failed to identify any wheelbase-related issues. The configuration was deemed so good in fact that the Renault 4 was not the only model of the marque to have a similar arrangement.

Engine Choice

Following extensive tests using various types of engines – air-cooled, water-cooled, various numbers of cylinders, in-line, transverse, horizontally opposed and even two-strokes – it was evident that, in order to keep within budget, little could beat the engine they already had in the 4CV but the question remained: how to make it drive the front wheels?

With the 4CV's water-cooled engine lifted from the rear and positioned in the front of the new car, it became clear that the original gearbox was far too long and with the gearchange mechanism emerging through the front of the casing, it meant that the donor's transmission couldn't be reused. The Renault designers took a deep breath and came up with a completely new, short and compact gearbox and final drive specifically for the Renault R4. It had an external splined drive on each side for connecting the driveshafts to the front wheels and a top-mounted gearchange lever. The engine sat behind the transmission near the bulkhead, with the gearbox and final drive poking out towards the front, just behind the grille, and the gearchange lever pointing upwards. At a stroke the R4 had now become the first of Renault's long list of front-wheel drive passenger cars.

This unusual arrangement of the power unit necessitated an imaginative but brilliantly simple design for the gear linkage, and a 2CV-style, through-the-dashboard mechanism was devised although unlike its rival, it also passed across the top of the engine – a very French but effective solution. Having the gearbox in front of an inline engine was certainly nothing new; the Citroën DS and its immediate predecessor both had this layout. There is no doubt it provides a benefit in weight distribution but in the case of the new Renault this was just a useful side effect; it meant there was no gear lever cluttering the space between the front seats.

Following a trip through the sawmill, this 1961 base model rather conveniently reveals some of its details. Notice the hammock or deckchair-style seat frames and coverings, absence of door cards, simple slot interior door catches and the metal coolant expansion tank fitted in the right-hand wing. The lack of rear suspension intrusion is also evident with the horizontal rear telescopic dampers being visible. (Renault)

Engine layout of an early R4. With a 6-volt system, a dynamo, an early jack and a metal coolant expansion tank neatly secreted inside the right-hand wing, it can be no later than 1965. As expected, it has the early, diagonally braced bonnet with the smaller grille aperture. The simple yet effective 'up-and-over' gear linkage, which lasted virtually unchanged throughout the model's life and engages with the level sprouting from the top of the box, can also be seen. (Author)

The early type of dashboard with the three-spoke steering wheel and the crackle finish to the heater unit complete with the first type of fresh-air vent levers and flaps. The delicate-looking rear-view mirror is dash-mounted and would remain so in one form or another until 1983. What is also apparent is the lack of a sun visor, even for the driver. Note that there has also been virtually no attempt to hide the various fixings; screws, nuts and bolts are all proudly on show. (Renault)

One oddity with using the 4CV engine as described was related to the use of a starting handle, still considered at the time to be an essential fitment especially with six-volt electrics. With the engine now effectively swapped around and the drive dog refitted to the other end of the engine, the starting handle would now have to be turned anticlockwise. This was unnatural and deemed unacceptable, and so in another fairly radical move the unit was re-engineered to run in the other direction. This fact wasn't always fully understood further down the line however, and using the motor from either a 4CV or Dauphine in an early R4 would result in three reverse gears but only a single forward one.

Innovation and Design

It might have been a small and basic car only intended to provide functional transport but the Renault 4 was certainly not short of technical firsts and design features, all intended to add to the usability and cost-effectiveness of ownership with a reduced need for very regular servicing.

In order to counter any suggestion that the use of water rather than air cooling would lead to more maintenance, the cooling system was sealed and fitted with a metal expansion tank under the right front wing, although later in the model's development it was replaced by firstly a glass bottle but then a plastic version inside the engine compartment. This set-up was a first for any car, banishing virtually for life coolant loss and the need for regular top-ups. There cannot be any motor vehicle today that doesn't benefit from this innovation and the Renault 4 was genuinely the pioneer. In designing the suspension and steering, the team also fitted it with sealed-for-life ball joints and track rod ends, meaning that regular greasing would also be consigned to history. Again, this was virtually unheard of at the time and many other cars still had nipples needing regular attention well into the 1980s. With the carrying of varying loads that the car and its compliant suspension encouraged, the headlights could potentially dazzle oncoming traffic, so a simple manual adjustment lever for each bulb was incorporated in the lamp carriers.

Despite monocoque construction becoming popular in the 1950s, the Renault 4 designers reverted to a platform chassis, or semi-monocoque. This led to the vulnerable but largely unstressed bodywork being bolted-on allowing not only quicker and cheaper repairs but manufacturing flexibility with saloons, vans, pick-ups, and other derivatives all being straightforward to produce. Access to the rear luggage space was provided via a top-hinged full-height boot lid, thus forming one of the first hatchbacks. The loadspace was further enhanced by either drop-down or removable rear seats depending on the specific model, turning the four-seater saloon car into a useful van-like vehicle.

The doors too had some nice touches. The internal catches simply took the form of a slot into the inner void so one could reach the mechanism and give it the necessary squeeze to release the door, saving even more money in development and production of internal handles; the rear doors too were usefully shaped to provide headroom as one got in or out. The Citroën had horizontally hinged windows providing a slightly awkward low opening, and they could drop closed at the most inopportune moment. Renault didn't stretch to

A base R3 or R4 at rest on a rural road somewhere in France, possibly during some kind of test. It doesn't have the feel of a marketing shot although the registration number does looks like a made-up one. The blanked-out side rear quarter panels are all too obvious along with the early fuel filler, bumpers and absence of hubcaps. There's no sunroof but the lack of leaves on the trees may point to the colder months. I'll bet the occupants were pleased that Renault fitted every version of the car with a heater. (Renault)

wind-ups – that would have broken their budget – but they fitted sliding windows instead with some versions getting rear ones as well. They still didn't open fully but they were big enough to allow the occupants to poke out their head. All of the glass including the windscreen was flat, which certainly wasn't fashionable at the time – many cars of the era were being designed with wrap-around front and rear windows and even curved side glass – but it was cheaper and perfectly functional.

Prototypes

To help keep within financial constraints, Dreyfus made sure his basic concepts were fully understood before any running prototypes were built. Some of the styling exercises and even the test vehicles could not be considered attractive, although most of them bore some features and hallmarks that would later surface in the final product. The first example had very angular doors and a heavy C pillar but the trademark grille, front wing definition and rear hatch were all evident. Later test cars would look much more familiar and, as project 112 progressed, they would begin to look unmistakably Renault 4. The body shape was deliberately boxy and

A quite early, classic three-view, coloured drawing of one of the proposals for Project 112. Some signs of Renault 4 are evident with the rear door shape, top-hinged tailgate and side swage line, but it seems to adopt a somewhat tail-heavy stance. (Renault)

A fairly early but fully painted and finished clay model of a prototype Project 112. It is probably quarter-scale in size and would be used to determine if the design worked and should be built as a full-size running version. While it is clearly not a model of the final design, there is no doubt it has certain similarities to the eventual car but with a rather fussy front bumper treatment. (Renault)

A running prototype of the Renault 4, or more correctly for the time, Project 112, on test. It is fairly close now to the final design, close enough to make comparisons with the Fiat 600 and a Citroën 2CV in hot pursuit. The latter incidentally has the first type of three-part bonnet and wings rather than the one-piece ripple bonnet fitted to very early examples. Bringing up the rear, with the roof rack, is a Renault Frégate Domaine test support vehicle. (Renault)

encompassed both front and rear wheels – the days of cars having separate and space-wasteful wings with narrow bodies and reduced inside space were over. The design team reasoned that, given a certain size of vehicle, the way to provide the maximum internal space was to use rectangular boxes as the basic design. It wouldn't be pretty but the new car wasn't setting out to win a *concours d'elégance*; it just had to be roomy and functional.

The Renault 4 development programme was shrouded in secrecy and in an attempt to keep it so for as long as possible, the remote test drivers reported back to base using coded telegrams. One dated November 1959 reads *'Marie Chantal et ses enfants envoient tous leurs meilleurs voeux a leurs parents'*, or 'Marie Chantal and her children send their best wishes to their parents'. The source of the sender has been censured to keep the test location secure, and 'Marie Chantal' was the codename of the car. Within three years, prototypes of the final Renault 4 were being put through their paces across the world from the USA to Sweden, via Sardinia and Guinea. During testing, nearly 200 million miles were covered and the drivers made it their mission to try to break the new car. Would the torsion bars snap? Would the sealed cooling system boil? The testing regime gave the team ample opportunity to ensure that the novel technological solutions worked and would remain reliable in the hands of owners.

Into Production

On 6 July 1961 the last 4CV rolled out of Boulogne-Billancourt ready for manufacture of the new Renault 4. Miraculously, within just four weeks the workforce had dismantled the old production lines and set up the new ones. In characteristic fashion, Dreyfus planned the entire operation down to the finest detail, with a thousand workers and 400 contract

A proud father with his baby. Pierre Dreyfus is understandably very pleased with his creation, which was by that stage proving very successful. From the hubcaps, sliding rear windows, the flat bumpers and the smaller grille, it's an R4L model dating between 1963 and 1967. The Renault R16 in the background however gives the game away and means the photo can be no earlier than 1965. (Renault)

staff staying behind as the factory closed for the traditional French summer holidays. New machinery and updated production lines were installed, along with the associated stores and workshops. Over 200,000 man-hours later and, exactly on schedule as the holidays ended, the reconfiguration was finished and on 3 August 1961, the first batch of Renault 4s rolled out of the factory. It had taken five years from that initial concept for a 4CV replacement but now the new Renault was ready to face the world.

Launching the Renault 4

Just how a new car is introduced to both the press and public alike can really make a big difference to sales, certainly in the first few months. Journalists are important because what they think and write will inevitably influence the car-buying public, but it is those customers who really matter, long after the magazines and newspapers have been read and discarded. Pierre Dreyfus knew that, just like Lefaucheux had done for the 4CV, they really had to do something special to make sure Renault 4 would become engrained in the psyche of potential owners and he had quite an event planned... but more of that later.

As early as March 1961 – six months before the official launch – an event codenamed Opération Soraya was staged. This allowed certain carefully chosen dealerships to get a sneak preview. A film recording of the session begins in the courtyard of a chateau on a misty spring morning with the arrival of several coachloads of participants. With a cloak of absolute secrecy under a Gendarme guard, they were invited to try the new car out on varying and challenging surfaces, all in the privacy of the secluded chateau. The Renault 4 was introduced to the press six months later with a week in the Camargue region in southern France near Saintes-Maries-de-la-Mer, where thirty cars of various specifications were made available for testing over a variety of carefully chosen roads. Besides being rather pleasant, the location was sparsely populated with few locals taking even the slightest interest in the myriad little cars being thrashed around. Apart from a few journalist-initiated breakages and crashes, the cars stood up well and, despite news remaining embargoed until the official launch date, very favourable reports would be forthcoming.

The German Motor Show opened a week ahead of the Paris Salon, thus giving Dreyfus the opportunity to stress that the new Renault was intended for all markets, and not just France alone. The Renault 4 was officially unveiled at the International Motor Show (IAA) in Frankfurt during the last week of September 1961, its French debut following a week later with a press reception at the Palais de Chaillot. French motorists got to see the car at the Paris Salon the very next day when a van and three saloon versions, the R3, the R4 and the R4L, were launched simultaneously. The L meant luxury and it's this specific model which was soon taken to the French public's hearts and resulted in all Renault R4s, and even R3s, acquiring the generic moniker 'La Quatrelle'.

General de Gaulle was present at the launch and showed a great interest in the new car. He approached Michelin, the then owners of Citroën, and asked how they were getting on at the show. When they claimed that Renault had copied their 2CV, even down to the seat design, Dreyfus took great satisfaction in pointing out that the new Renault was actually a much better car in a variety of areas, and that those seats had been patented by Renault before the war. The compliant and long-travel suspension was a significant feature and

A very early 603 cc Renault R3 almost certainly dating from the first few weeks of production. It still has the original low position of fuel filler, which on harsh cornering led to fuel loss through the vent hole in the cap – most were corrected under warranty within a few weeks. Oddly, and perhaps indicating it's a press car, this very basic model has the optional (and quite expensive) fabric sunroof. Also evident are the external door hinges and the very early type of tailgate fixings. (Renault)

a display rig was set up comprising an open chassis with seating and driving controls, running on a bumpy rolling road. Visitors were encouraged to sit inside and examine the suspension hard at work absorbing the ups and downs of the undulating road surface while they enjoyed the smooth and undisturbed ride.

The new Renault was accepted immediately; the French loved the idea of a comfortable utilitarian car with acceptable performance and excellent load-carrying capability. Simple mechanics and minimal maintenance were added bonuses. Pierre Dreyfus was now ready to stage his special event to seal the Quatrelle into potential owners' minds. On the day after the public launch, a fleet of car transporters took 200 new cars onto the streets of Paris. With 'Prenez le volant' written on the sides and the keys left in the ignition, potential customers were invited to 'take the wheel'. With cars lined up in the shadow of the Eiffel Tower and the others dotted all over the French capital, the Renaults could be seen exploring every nook and cranny of the city. During the ten days of this masterstroke of marketing, around a quarter of a million miles were covered at the hands of some 60,000 drivers and, in terms of initial sales, it proved to be a hugely successful operation. Similar exercises took place in other parts of Europe including The Netherlands, Germany and Belgium. In February 1962 a small fleet of white R4Ls with a label on the windscreen, 'Stop that car – this is the Remarkable R4', arrived in Britain and gave local drivers a chance to experience the Renault for themselves.

Voila! La Quatrelle est arrivée!

On the day following the launch in 1961, 200 R4Ls with a *Prenez le volant* sticker on the wing, keys in the ignition and a trio of red, white and blue pennants with one declaring *essai libre* or 'free trial' were dotted around Paris and many potential customers did indeed 'take the wheel'. Some of the cars here are neatly parked in the shadow of the Eiffel Tower awaiting their tests. Similar but more low-key events took place over the forthcoming months in various other European countries including Britain. (Renault)

A very early Renault 4 van – the F4 or Fourgonnette. The F4 was based on the same floor pan as the saloon and was virtually identical from the B pillar forward. Small panel vans were very popular not only in France but in many other countries and the F4 and its derivatives lasted well into the 1980s and, in certain markets, the early 1990s. (Renault)

4

Through the Decades

To say the Renault 4 was well received by the French public is a bit of an understatement. After the reveal at the Paris Salon and the try-before-you-buy event, sales were buoyant. The combination of low purchase price, simple maintenance, plenty of inside room

Another factory shot of the Renault 4 that very neatly shows the room for both passengers and their luggage. It has the opening rear quarter windows, and the 'tripod' hubcaps usually reserved for the Super, but not the bottom-hinged tailgate with opening window or double-bar chrome bumpers, so it might be an evaluation exercise for various trims and options. The low fuel filler of the very early cars is still evident. (Renault)

and a large, 17-cubic foot boot – nearly tripled with the rear seat folded – plus smooth performance and a supple ride, took the nation by storm. Although it was certainly similar in basic concept to the 2CV, it was more of a 'proper' car with a four-cylinder water-cooled engine instead of the raucous air-cooled, two-cylinder unit. The final clincher were the low reported running costs with contemporary adverts sounding: *'Pas de graissage, pas d'eau, juste un peu d'essence'*.

The base model R4 and R3 were ostensibly similar. While specific details varied according to their final destination, they had basic deckchair-style seating and were only available in grey with similarly finished bumpers and a pressed-out grille. Instead of a fuel gauge, they had a low-fuel warning light and a dipstick. They also missed out on hubcaps, windscreen washers, headlining, door cards, a key-operated ignition switch and even the rear quarter windows of its posher sibling. In the case of the R3, an asthmatic 603 cc engine designed to slot into the lower 3CV French taxation class was fitted whereas the R4 and R4Ls were fitted with the more reasonable 747 cc unit. The R3 was rarely offered outside the home market and, while very cunningly priced just below the cheapest Citroën 2CV, even the most impecunious French buyers willing to stand a certain level of

Austerity motoring! An interior shot of Mikaël Peyre's 1961 R4 (number 29 off the line). Note the lack of a proper headliner, missing door cards and large expanses of grey-painted metal. The very early type of dashboard, ventilation controls and three-spoke steering wheel are also on display. The (single) sun visor is almost certainly an option too but an essential fitment in le Midi. What one won't see here by the way is a fuel gauge – it didn't have one. (Peyre)

With the R3 and the very early R4, one didn't have the luxury of a fuel gauge but there was a low-tank level warning light fitted. Renault very thoughtfully provided a dipstick in the form of a calibrated bent metal strip, and a snippet from the owner's manual shows how to use the sophisticated device. Given this owner still has the low fuel filler prone to leakage on cornering, they probably had to dip the tank more frequently than they might have thought. (Renault & Peyre)

Very early Renault 4s had the fuel filler mounted very low causing petrol to escape via the cap's vent hole and within a month or two of launch, a recall was issued to fix the problem. Quite why this basic snag was not spotted during development is not recorded. In this pre-restoration shot, the factory's correction is clear but, in the interests of total originality, the owner of this car has since put the filler back to its low position – with the inevitable result. (Peyre)

austerity couldn't be tempted to save a few more francs, with the result that the R3 was soon dropped. The lack of C-pillar glass too was so generally unpopular that within a year or two all models were fully glazed.

The gear lever sprouting through the dashboard à la 2CV was novel but drivers soon mastered it. What they weren't so pleased about however was just three gears and no synchromesh on first. With windscreen wipers that didn't park, non-cancelling indicators and six-volt electrics, even the luxury 4L model was equipped with *necessary* rather than *nice-to-have* kit. Conversely, at a time when it was still an extra on many British cars, a heater was standard on all R4s. Fresh-air was available via the scuttle flaps and the optional folding roof let the sun flood in – perfect for the Côte d'Azur.

In the meantime, Citroën realised there was a need for a more upmarket and slightly bigger car than their 2CV and, six months before the Renault 4, launched the Ami 6. The distinctively styled new model with its reverse-slope or 'Breezeway' rear window helped fill the size and price gap between the 2CV and the DS/ID, a much bigger and more expensive

A very early Fourgonnette – early enough to have the erroneously positioned low fuel filler. On the saloon the warranty fix would be relatively simple but here the entire panel was affected and presumably some kind of filler section would have been employed. Note the novel, and exclusive to Renault, top opening which operates independently of the rear door and proved very useful for carrying long loads. Not without some humour is it referred to as the *girafon*, or giraffe hatch. (Renault)

Another interior shot of Mikaël Peyre's 1961 R4. The very basic hammock or deckchair-style seating is evident, along with the rubber floor covering. Note the finger slot in the interior door skin to operate the catch. The seat is very easily removed to either increase luggage space or to provide a handy outside perch. This 4 is proving as practical as ever, and has been photographed returning from a produce collecting mission – presumably the compliant, long-travel suspension has meant that very few, if any, have been lost. (Peyre)

car. With similar interlinked coil and leading arm suspension of the smaller car but with an enlarged 602 cc version of the air-cooled flat-twin, Citroën had correctly surmised that a Renault 4CV successor was imminent and reacted accordingly, doubtless causing *un petit mal de tête* at Boulogne-Billancourt...

The Renault 4 in Britain

With Renault intent on selling the new car to as many countries as possible, it was inevitable the R4 would come to these shores, but would British buyers take to it? Front-wheel drive was becoming fashionable with BMC's Mini and 1100, and probably helped remove some of the fear of buying foreign. The space, comfort and promise of low running costs too was certainly appreciated with local advertising echoing, 'No greasing, no water and just a little petrol', and with the car being referred to as 'The Remarkable Renault 4'.

One of the first motoring magazines to try the Renault 4 was *Autocar* and on 30 March 1962 wrote: 'This car has few pretensions as a status symbol, its performance is marginal, and it is obvious that no artistic stylist spent sleepless nights pondering on

Country cousins!

Renault 4 – the go-anywhere do-anything town-and-country car.

This is the kind of car you can drive anywhere to do anything. For toughness and reliability, it's in a class on its own.

Being rugged, good-looking and comfortable all at once is the Renault 4's secret, so draw closer. First, there's the suspension. Independent all round with torsion bars. Then there's a tough box frame chassis, front wheel drive, and comfortable deep foam seats to complete the picture.

A very beautiful one it is too. An elegant five door family saloon entirely accustomed to entertaining busloads of passengers. The door at the back swings up while you load up royal volumes of luggage.

Even The Times was impressed to note that: 'It swallowed a 5 foot sofa which a vast American shooting brake had been unable to accommodate.'

The Renault 4 boasts certain other practical advantages. Like 40-45 to the gallon. No greasing to pay for. No anti-freeze to buy because it's already sealed in the cooling system. And servicing is reduced to the absolute minimum. To save you money.

Look up a country cousin and go for a ride.

Renault 4—£612. De Luxe version £643 (both inc. p.t. ex. works).

Write to Renault Limited, Western Avenue, London, W.3 for free Renault 4 brochure and list of nearest dealers.

One of Renault's magazine adverts for the British market and dating from 1968 or 1969 judging by the 'G' registration. It was either optimistic or clever, but certainly tongue-in-cheek, to refer to a tractor, a Land Rover and the R4 as 'Country cousins'. With a cottage in the background and the odd chicken clucking around the drive, the very happy-looking lady in the straw hat has the choice of the perfect vehicle for the job. While not having so much in common, the R4 and the Land Rover both had manually deployed scuttle ventilation systems. (Renault & Author's collection)

The R3 in Renault's own collection. The Renault Classic collection includes more than 760 vehicles and (to quote): 'illustrates the inventiveness and know-how of the company founded in 1898 in Boulogne-Billancourt'. Unfortunately the collection is not usually open to the public. (Renault)

A midlife Renault 4 in a very rural setting. This one still retains the side-exit exhaust of the earlier cars and it has curved chrome bumpers. Having the full-width aluminium grille and a metal scuttle vent but still with the starting handle hole dates this one to somewhere between 1968 and 1971. By this time all non-basic variants had the luxury of opening rear side windows. If we could see the rear of the car, it would have the second version of hatch hinges which were bolted on, not welded on like the earliest type. (Vos)

A Renault 4 'Safari' limited edition on the production line and dating the image to between 1975 to 1979. Based on the standard model with the 782 cc engine, it had rubber side strips, multicoloured fabric seats with padded knee supports, satin black exterior trim and the steering wheel from the Renault 5. None of the special editions were officially sold in Britain. From the contents of the conveyer and the operation being performed, this area must be the seat-fitting bay, possibly in the Boulogne-Billancourt factory. (Renault)

In a carefully contrived setting almost certainly devised to appeal to a certain sector of the UK market, there is no doubting the Renault's practicality and ability to perform the kind of work suggested. Even the Labrador is present and I bet those wellies are green. The Quatrelle has been pressed into all kinds of service and duties throughout its sixty years. (Renault)

this venture.' Later: 'The car can be driven at incredible speed over severe undulations and through deep pot-holes while remaining almost on an even keel.' One of the *Autocar* test team suggested that it was a combination of the smooth suspension and the extremely simple and well-designed seats alone which made the car an 'extraordinarily attractive proposition'. After suggesting the Renault was most suitable for either French motorists or those in various colonial markets, they rather harshly concluded that to consider that it would sell well in the United Kingdom would have been the remark of a real optimist.

Three months later, *Motor Sport* was more positive, seeming to understand the intention of the car and the headline 'What fun! How Practical!' was to bode well. The tester admitted that after 700 miles of driving this 'elementary but essentially practical Renault', he was a convert. He said, 'The use of a well-tried four-cylinder engine rather than a phutter-phut twin, imparts the smoothness, quietness and performance expected of a normal small car to this fascinating new vehicle for farmers and other non-snobs.' He added, 'The suspension renders the 4L impervious to unmade surfaces and rutted lanes and it rides over bumps, ruts, level-crossings and the like in complete comfort.' Predictably perhaps for a sporty publication,

A fairly early R4L, now with a ribbed bonnet – so not very early, but it does still have the original type of small radiator grille and tubular (chrome) bumpers. Like many 4s of this age it doesn't have rear side opening windows but it does have the hinged rear quarter glass. With these features, as well as the wide chrome strip beneath the doors and tripod hubcaps, it's from 1963 or slightly earlier. (Vos)

One of the Renault magazine adverts described a similar version to this one thus: 'This is not just a car! It's a miracle. Holds five. Holds their luggage. Holds any road, anywhere. Costs £540!' Then the message went on to say it was down-to-earth, practical, versatile and economical. After all the usual stuff about no greasing points and a sealed-for-life cooling system (forget antifreeze!), it was claimed it had 'town and country horns' too. (Author)

A base model Renault 4. It is a slightly later one with a ribbed bonnet and flat bumpers. All basic models as well as the commercials in a similar trim level had painted headlight surrounds, no hubcaps and a simple pressed metal radiator grille. To the uninitiated, it is very easy and almost forgivable to confuse an R4 as an R3, and vice versa. (Author)

Another view of a very early – number 29 off the line in fact – Renault R4 in yet another rural setting and complete with yet another horse. Spot the very early type of flat bonnet with its diagonal bracing just visible through the simple pressed metal grille slots. (Peyre)

he had fun because he said with a little confidence the 4L could be hurled around corners at a 'fine angle of lean', while its tyres 'squeaked with glee'. One photo caption in the report reads: 'Practical but not exactly pretty.' He was encouraging in his conclusion though, pointing out that the world would be a poorer place without these ingenious and practical people's-cars. Having then said – possibly correctly – that very few of their press-on driver readers would want one, he added: 'If you require a car-cum van, or just regard space and comfort as more important in an economy car than speed, you cannot ignore this cocky newcomer from the great Billancourt plant.' He finished: 'For comfort, economy and spaciousness, coupled with freedom from servicing worries, the Renault 4L is remarkable.'

Early Adoption

Just two years into service, the R4L acquired the bigger Billancourt 845 cc engine derived from that in the Dauphine, giving it a worthwhile improvement in performance. The power had only increased by a couple of bhp to 28, but the torque was up 25 per cent from 40.5 to 49 lb-ft, trimming six seconds off the zero to 40 mph time and increasing the top speed from 54 to an autoroute-friendly 70 mph. The three speeds remained, although they were now all fully synchronised which made town driving much easier. An *Autocar* test in November 1963 maintained its praise of the ride comfort but also the criticism of the fascia and the layout of the minor controls, with the closing comment: 'Renault have taken the view that if it works it does not matter what it looks like.' That same year, a Super version was available in certain markets with double-bar chrome bumpers, better seats, opening rear quarter windows and a bottom-hinged boot lid with a slide-down rear window – not unlike the large American station wagons of the time.

Often being a second car, the marketing people at Renault decided to make the R4 appeal to the fashionable, about-town, modern woman. They used *Elle* magazine, one of the top publications aimed at just the readership they hoped to tap into, and in early 1963 launched the *'Elle prend le volant!'*, or the 'She's driving!' campaign. This was aimed at introducing female customers to the chic and glamorous Renault 4, and drivers had forty-eight hours to test drive the car and judge its qualities. Following an assessment of the feedback, an initial batch of 500 Super models were transformed into the 'Parisienne', with black paint

A fully dressed R4 Super! The owner of this one is clearly very proud and has splashed out on virtually every accessory from the catalogue: mudflaps complete with lozenge logo, chrome door handle escutcheons, chrome wheel arch trims, sunroof and so on – and they're just the ones we can see. What might not be clear is that the rear bumper was hinged to clear the tailgate. The slide-down rear glass on the Super would be very welcome in the hot weather. (Vos)

The remarkable RENAULT 4

EXCEPTIONAL CAPACITY — AMAZING COMFORT AND SUSPENSION — INCREDIBLE ECONOMY
NO GREASING WHATSOEVER — PERMANENTLY SEALED COOLING SYSTEM

Typical of the time, this illustration was used in various early brochures for the R4, and in many different markets. The R4 specific magazine *4L* have located the setting as Sonchamp in France. It is very close to Château Porgès de Rochefort-en-Yvelines used by Renault for the dealer launch Opération Soraya, and around 25 miles from the Renault test centre at Lardy. (Renault)

The black Parisienne models were available with either gold cane wickerwork, or (slightly oddly for Paris) green or red Scottish tartan. Peter Sellers rather famously had a Mini Cooper extensively modified by renowned coachbuilders Hooper and finished in Royal Purple with a hand-painted wicker pattern. Since Seller's Mini was completed around the same time in early 1963, did one inspire the other? (Renault)

Aimed unashamedly at the female driver, the 'Parisienne' model launched in 1963 was initially based on a black Super. Renault used *Elle* magazine with a suitable campaign to expand into a new market. Perhaps the success of the Mini with Carnaby Street and various high-profile celebrities had fed into a marketing meeting at Boulogne-Billancourt? This is a recently taken photo of a beautifully original 1964 Parisienne slotted into a very rural setting – possibly not quite what Renault had in mind for the specific version but it now seems appropriate. (De Comtes)

RENAULT 4L

pas d'eau, pas de graissage, juste un peu d'essence

In a lovely period advert for one of the early flat-bonnet R4Ls, this group of friends look very happy despite apparently being lost; did they plan to end up on a beach? Quite how six full-sized adults fit into even the impressively roomy Renault is anyone's guess but maybe the optional sunroof helps. Note the oft-quoted strapline regarding coolant, grease and petrol, but there was another one that frequently cropped up: 'Allez-y … vous êtes en R4!', or 'Go ahead … you are in an R4!' (Renault)

R4s being built in the Boulogne-Billancourt plant around 1963 or 1964. The shells have reached the 'Body-in-White' stage where the completed shell is ready for paint and before anything else (mechanics, electrics, trim, etc.) has been added. They are undergoing a few final smoothing operations prior to cleaning and priming. Not much in the way of PPE is evident but all of the operatives are wearing the dungaree which was, and still is, a popular protective garment of choice on the Continent. (Renault)

A factory shot showing the bottom-hinged tailgate and slide-down rear window which would later become the main feature of the Super model. This car also has the now much sought-after tripod hubcaps and opening rear quarter windows. Being a non-base model, the seats are better upholstered and look a little more inviting than the hammock style. Note the keys left in the catch – a sure way to damage the surrounding paintwork. (Renault)

And here we have a Super model in all its glory on a sunny day in a poplar-lined avenue somewhere in rural France. Despite the fancy double-bar chrome bumpers, the drop-down rear window and opening rear quarter lights, one can be in no doubt about the models' nomenclature with the chrome 'Renault 4 Super' script. Being slightly later than launch, this car also has its fuel filler mounted higher to avoid spillage. (Renault)

and either a gold cane pattern or a Scottish tartan in green or red, and modelled by the French pop singer Sheila, later known in the UK as Sheila B Devotion with the modest 1979 hit 'Spacer'. The Parisienne version of the R4 was a success and, with further slight variations, it lasted until 1968.

Milestone

In 1965 the Régie decided that the R4 would officially become the 'Renault 4' with the 'R' being dropped. On 1 February the following year, the million mark was reached matching the success of the 4CV after just over four years. Headline writers on this side of the Channel didn't stay silent: '1 Million people (and their families) prefer this car to any other!' By this time more than 10,000 had found homes in Britain. A further year on and the car finally received the much-needed extra gear and, with 370,000 being built each year, it became France's best-selling car. The Renault 4 didn't change much over the years but, in late 1967, it did get a facelift and its grille, still polished aluminium, now enveloped the headlights.

The first million Renault 4s were produced by 1 February 1966, less than four and a half years after its launch. Here the inevitable and well-earned marketing event celebrates the momentous occasion while enthusiastic workers look on. (Minney)

1 Million people
(and their families)
prefer <u>this</u> car to any other!

1,000,000 Renault 4's have been produced
since its introduction less than 4½ years ago–a record
unequalled by any other European manufacturer

Over ten thousand Renault 4's have already been sold in Great Britain and it is the best selling car in France today.

The Renault 4 is the most comfortable, economical and lowest priced 4-door Estate Car on the market.

The ideal car for family and business the Renault 4 needs no greasing, does 40-50 m.p.g. and includes heater, screen washer, etc. There are 400 distributors and dealers throughout the country for parts and after-sales service.

Write to us for full details and name of your nearest dealer or post this coupon.
Renault 4 £548.18.9d. (inc. p.t.)
Renault Limited, Western Avenue, London W.3

RENAULT 4

Name_____

Address_____

_____

Present car owned_____

CVS–543

The production of one million R4s didn't go unnoticed around the world and here in a British advert, the point is made quite succinctly in the headline. It goes on to say that 10,000 of the million had been sold here and declared it to be 'the most comfortable, economical and cheapest four-door estate car on the market'. Praise indeed! (Author's collection)

At the start of the new decade and with production in South America, Australia and many European countries, the Renault 4 was now considered a genuine World Car. Minor development adjustments continued with 12 volts being adopted and, in 1974 with the growing trend away from brightwork, a plastic grille was fitted. A couple of years later and the Safari limited edition was added with its bright body colours and unique trim being aimed at a younger market. By 1977 Renault had become Europe's biggest car manufacturer, with five million 4s having been produced.

For the British market the available models were now the L and the TL, with the latter gaining improved fascia and seats. *Autocar* tested the TL in 1977 and clearly now had

This is the engine compartment from a midlife R4. It has the glass coolant expansion bottle with an engine-driven fan and a 12-volt battery (but it's still up by the bulkhead). It retains a dynamo and regulator box, but has acquired the later version of (parallelogram) jack, dating the car between 1971 to 1975. Although not obvious, it would by now have four fully synchronised gears. Note the gear linkage across the top of the rocker cover. (Renault)

some affection for the Renault 4 and despite the changes noted: 'The abiding character of this lovable maid-of-all-work remains happily unchanged.' And the new seats: 'Plush, modern affairs, but the delightful versatility of instant conversion into estate car remains as valuable as ever.' They also said the 'ghastly' old fascia had been improved and tidied up. The following year, and certainly for the British market, the L was replaced by the TL, and a new GTL version was introduced. In other countries trim levels were naturally adjusted to suit the local demand. The GTL was more upmarket and was fitted with the 1108 cc Cléon-Fonte engine from the Renault 6, the TL receiving the similar 956 cc unit a few years later (although in the UK the TL retained the 845 cc lump). The GTL's engine was detuned to achieve economy (one of its raison d'être features) and, with higher gearing and an improvement in torque from the larger unit, 60–65 mph cruising was now possible. It also gained self-cancelling indicators, hazard warning lights, plastic door claddings, grey painted bumpers and 'bumperettes' – forward-facing tubular loops between the wings and front panel, first fitted to the facelift models of 1967 and called 'Buffalo Bars' by Renault. The luxury of a heated rear window had been available from the mid-1970s.

Another picture of the Body-in-White stage but this time the shells are the later type to suit the plastic grilles and rectangular front lights. The factory shown is on the Ivory Coast, West Africa, near the port of Abidjan and independent from France since 1960. Two years later, the Renault-Africa Regional Division created the Société Africaine de Fabrication des Automobiles Renault (SAFAR). The Renault 4 and the Renault company itself played a key role in the support of developing nations. (Renault)

Another image that demonstrates the global nature of Renault, these R4s are being assembled in Portugal. In the early 1960s, imports of complete cars into the country were banned and so in late 1963 Industrias Lustitanias Renault (ILR) at Guarda, 150 miles north-east of Lisbon, was opened to assemble Renaults using local labour. The Portuguese and the Spanish took to the R4 and many can still be seen doing what they do best, ferrying people and things around the Iberian Peninsula and the related islands. With Renault 5s sharing the track, this scene dates from at least 1972. (Renault)

The French Gendarmerie Nationale selected both saloon and van versions of the Renault 4, more often than not painted in a very distinctive shade of mid-blue. Nearly 15,000 R4s joined the Gendarmerie from 1962 until the late 1980s, not least because it met one of their essential requirements that a person must be able to sit inside while wearing a *képi*, or a cap with a 'flat circular top and a peak, or visor', just like General Charles de Gaulle could often be seen wearing. (Renault)

The separate chassis of the R4 meant changing the body was relatively straightforward and in 1970 ACL (Ateliers de Construction du Livradois), in a partnership with Renault, produced the Rodeo, a Citroën Méhari competitor and designed mainly for recreational purposes. With four-wheel drive versions also available courtesy of Sinpar mechanics, there were three generations of the vehicle. It was withdrawn in 1987. (Renault)

As well as the more usual panelled R4 vans, the Fourgonnette could also be ordered with opening side windows. A removable rear seat was available as an option giving the owner the best possible choice between a van in the week and a car at the weekend. This one is being loaded with the morning's supply of bread along with the very necessary baguette display baskets. Note the very practical 'giraffe' flap at the top has been lifted to give a little extra room. (Renault)

The second type of dashboard arrangement. This was fitted between 1967 and 1982 but this one being finished in black rather than brown signifies it's 1974 or onwards. Contemporary road testers remained less than complimentary about the layout of the minor controls. Note the two-spoke steering wheel and the rear-view mirror still firmly screwed to the dash-top. Door pockets are evident along with the simple yet effective door check straps. (Renault)

68 This van is an EDF one. Électricité de France is the state-owned energy company, possessing an extensive fleet of Renaults for the smaller, more local jobs. It's not easy to see from this angle but it doesn't appear to have the top opening flap over the rear door. With the 4CV parked in the background, it may be a fairly early one. (Renault)

The French Post Office adopted the Renault 4 van as one of its first fleet vehicles and, like the one pictured here, they were painted in a standard shade of yellow – officially code '030', but more usually just referred to as Post Office Yellow. For many years they could be seen all over the country collecting and delivering letters, parcels and packages. (Vos)

The last type of dashboard which appeared in 1982. Now an expanse of plastic, the ergonomics have been marginally improved although the heater controls are still somewhat haphazardly arranged. The gear lever remains but now the instrument panel and steering wheel are basically those from the R5. While some of the character has been lost, the new fascia is much better than the earlier types and the rear-view mirror is now positioned where it should be. This is a GTL model with tartan cloth seats. (Renault)

The engine compartment from a 1986 1108 cc GTL. Notice the late type of jack, the plastic coolant expansion bottle, electric radiator fan, electric washer pump and 12-volt electrics (the battery is now further forward helping to avoid the brake master cylinder on a right-hand drive car). With a heated rear window as standard, no wonder it needed the now-standard fitment of an alternator. Spot the air intake hose from the air filter set in the cold weather position to pick up warm air from the exhaust manifold. (Author)

A fairly late Fourgonnette; the grey plastic grille, bumperettes and black plastic scuttle vent mean it must be from at least 1983. This van also has the small side window and is parked in a typically French setting. (Renault)

Another shot of the late-style, R5-inspired, interior. This GTL model has a proper headlining and twin sun visors but still has a very practical rubber floor covering. The heater unit, though fundamentally unchanged, is now slightly more tucked away behind the fascia. While there is an ashtray in the middle of the front face of the dash, the two flaps by the base of the windscreen are not additional used cigarette repositories but the internal outlets for the wonderfully effective scuttle ventilation system. (Author)

Some cars look terrible if they are not absolutely immaculate but the Renault 4, like its Citroën counterpart, wears patination and the knocks and scrapes from an honest life very well. This shabby but chic example is still in daily use and was captured parked in a side street in Mytilene, the capital of the Greek island of Lesbos. (Smith)

With very few indigenous vehicle manufacturers, Denmark had to source cars and vans from other countries and the postal service was no exception. This Danish stamp of 10 Krone (about £1) features a 1984 Renault F4 in Danish postal livery and was issued in 2002 as part of a Delivery Vehicles commemorative series. (Karsholt)

By the time the 1980s arrived, the Renault 4 was clearly outdated and outclassed by its rivals, but remained in demand in many countries with 1,500 produced every day. This figure was almost the same as that on its launch twenty years earlier despite a specification that had remained virtually unchanged for well over a decade. With popularity never really waning, Renault seemed to take the view that while it was selling, it would keep making it. Within just a couple of weeks of each other, both *Autocar* and *Motor* magazines published

Above: In 1975 the Safari limited edition, based on the entry-level 782 cc model, was launched. It featured satin black bumpers, door handles and door mirrors, and a rubber bumper strip was stuck to each flank. Meant to attract a younger driver to the model, a wide choice of bright and cheerful colours was available. (Renault)

Left: The Safari had individual tubular front seats finished in a colourful multi-tone cloth and each was fitted with a built-in head restraint. (Renault)

The Jogging was launched in May 1981 to celebrate twenty years of the Renault 4. The advertising for the Jogging claimed that it was better than walking. This was a home-market advert, the model being only available in France and the Benelux countries. (Renault)

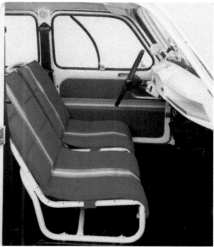

Above left: Again, aimed at younger drivers, the Jogging buyers were told: 'The car that wears sweat pants.' It boasted a huge canvas sunroof and a two-tone blue and white paint job with a rainbow-coloured stripe right around the car. Just to leave no one in any doubt, it also had 'Jogging' stickers on the bonnet and tailgate. (Renault)

Above right: Despite the standard 1108 cc GTL mechanicals underneath, both the seats and door trims were made to match the go-faster stripes on the outside. Slightly oddly, the seats had tubular frames similar to the very early ones in the original base-model 4s, although they were now white painted. As if that wasn't enough, the dashboard was also white, which surely led to dazzling on a sunny day. Lastly, every one of the 5,000 Jogging models came with a similarly stripey sports bag lodged in the boot. (Renault)

tests on the GTL. *Motor* wrote in February 1980: ' its limited passenger accommodation, its poor performance and standards of heating, ventilation, ergonomics, visibility, finish and equipment that would have seemed outdated in 1970; in 1980 they should be unacceptable'. They noted that given the GTL's excellent economy, its practicality, and an intangible asset they called character, the 4,000 Renault were planning to build that year would be easy to sell. The rest of the report was scattered with the usual criticism of what was by 1980 a very old design, but one detects respect and appreciation. *Autocar's* view was much the same.

By now it was obvious that the 4's days were numbered and, despite reasonable sales figures, Renault felt that limited editions would help maintain interest. In 1981 the 'Jogging' edition was launched with the 'Shopping' the year after, but limited to the Belgian market. Finally, a couple of years later, the 4 got the front disc brakes it needed plus a modified version of the dashboard and instruments from the Renault 5, including a windscreen-mounted rear-view mirror. Two further years on and the seven million point was reached. As if to celebrate, the 'Sixties' edition was created, a run of 2,200 blue, yellow or red GTLs with matt black bumpers and side trims, double-glass sunroofs plus jazzy seats. Towards the end of the decade, with a general move by Renault towards names instead of numbers, the 'Savane' and 'Clan' models replaced the TL and GTL respectively. In a final push for the younger market, the 'Carte Jeune' limited edition was offered and, based on the Savane, it featured unique colour and trim options. For the British market though, none of the special editions were available, just the TL and GTL models.

Still keen to draw in a younger crowd (have you spotted the theme yet?), the *Carte Jeunes* or 'Youth Card' edition was sprung on the French market in 1991. Based on the entry-level Savane specification, it was named after a government scheme to give young people easy and affordable transportation. Offered in red, yellow, white and dark green, it had a turquoise and blue stripe, logos and black seats with blue and green inserts. The special keyring that came with the car is very rare today and much sought after. (Renault)

Another limited edition not imported into Britain was the 'Sixties' of 1985. Based on the 1108 cc GTL and only available in yellow, blue and red, with colour-coordinated seats, two pop-up sunroofs and appropriate logos on the boot and wings, the run of 2,200 were sold very quickly. (Renault)

Size really does matter! This custom-built version of the R4 was a novel yet thoughtful attempt in the mid-1960s to solve some of the issues of city congestion. Engineering Consultant Jean Bertin realised that not only were smaller cars beneficial for congestion reduction and parking, but two or three of the seats were often empty and were therefore redundant. With nearly 30 inches sliced from the rear seating area the car design requirements were not only fully met but also the vital boot space remained intact. Even today, very few cars have adopted this now quite appealing solution. (Vos)

A 1986 1108 cc R4 GTL at rest. Notice the plastic side mouldings, grey-painted bumpers and door handles, full-length exhaust, and black plastic wheel nut and centre covers in place of hubcaps. The door hinges are now neatly tucked away inside the A and B pillars, and the tailgate hinges are the very late type. Finished in a non-original colour (for a mid-1980s car), it is clearly in fine fettle. (Author)

The separate platform chassis meant the R4 was a very useful donor vehicle. This particular example pictured at the Le Mans Classic is a sports car built by the French company SOciété des Véhicules André Morin (SOVAM). Visually rather distinctive, just 150 were built between 1965 and 1968. Another R4-based French special was the Tilbury, an open-topped sports car with looks reminiscent of a classic Morgan. A similarly low number were built over twenty years from 1986. (Miss)

The End

With stricter emissions and safety regulations, coupled with a relatively expensive build process requiring an excess of manual intervention rather than the favoured modern robot automation, the demise of the Renault 4 was inevitable. By the mid-1980s only the GTL model was available in Britain with none being imported into the country after 1987. The end of production was announced on 3 December 1992 with only two factories – Slovenia and Morocco – continuing, with the very last cars being built in 1994, when production finally officially ended. To salute the incredible success of the model a special edition farewell version was launched. With a run of just 1,000 cars, the 'Bye-Bye' had a unique numbered plaque on the dash – a rather low-key celebration of an amazing car. In April 1993 the all-new Twingo was launched replacing the 4 as the entry-level Renault.

Adieu la Quatrelle!

In 1992 after the announcement of the end of production of the Renault 4, a final limited edition was launched. Called the 'Bye-Bye', it was based on the GTL Clan but very little was added other than a numbered plaque attached to the dash. (Renault)

The numbered plaque was fitted just below the clock. This one is number 250 of the 1,000 Bye-Bye editions built. With the possibility of a brand-new and electric Renault 4, a 'see you again' farewell message like *Au Revoir* or *À Bientôt* may have been more appropriate. (Renault)

The R4 was as useful in the city as it was in the countryside. Here we have a Super parked outside the very famous and historic Cirque d'Hiver, or Winter Circus, in Paris. Dating back to 1852 the circus is famous because just seven years after its inception, Jules Léotard from Toulouse invented the flying trapeze act when he first leapt from one high-altitude swing to another. A young audience are about to leave their tripod hubcapped and double-bar-bumpered R4 to see the hopefully uplifting matinee performance. Not a parking meter in sight either. (Renault)

Introduced in Europe in 1993 in left-hand drive only and never officially available in the UK, the Twingo was the R4 replacement. At first, only one trim level and four colours were available with Indian Yellow on show here. With a colourful interior and chunky controls, it was intended to appeal to the younger customer and first editions now have classic status. This one has the optional full-length sunroof which, if one is handy with a jigsaw and pop-rivets, is a much-admired accessory for the R4 and easier to find than the original type. (Renault)

Pitched as an upmarket, bigger and more grown-up R4 to compete with the Citroën Ami 6 and Dyane, the Renault 6 of 1968 used a similar chassis and suspension with an 845 cc or (from 1970) a 45 bhp 1108 cc engine. It was nearly a decade before the R4 would enjoy the bigger unit, albeit in 'strangled' 34 bhp form. Today the bigger choke carb and matching inlet harvested from an old 6 are a much-prized quick tune-up kit to release just over 10 bhp extra from a GTL. (Author)

The Renault 5 was a three- or (later) a five-door 'Supermini' and was particularly successful in Europe where demand for this type of vehicle was very strong. Initially launched in 1972 using a similar torsion bar suspension set-up to the 4 and various engines depending on the specification, the model ran over two generations and twenty-five years. This is one of the earliest and very collectable versions. (Author)

5
Competitions and Expeditions

Unlike its predecessor, the 750, which acquired sporting credentials shortly after its introduction, the Renault 4 was never intended for motor sport. Its relatively low-powered engine, high centre of gravity and compliant suspension were not obvious qualities, and yet that very same long suspension travel, high-ground clearance and rugged dependability meant it would become an unexpected contender in rallying and long-distance expeditions.

East African Safari Rally

The Safari Rally was first held in 1953, as the East African Coronation Safari in Kenya, Uganda and Tanganyika, and celebrated the coronation of Queen Elizabeth II. In 1960 it was renamed the East African Safari Rally and kept that name until 1974, when it became the Kenya Safari Rally. Held on roads still open to the public, it proved notorious as one of the toughest rallies in the world with arduous conditions, constantly changing weather and around 3,500 competitive miles, so simply finishing was quite an achievement.

With the Renault 4 barely a year old, a dozen 4Ls were entered in the rally and as a mark of their ruggedness, the Madagascan team of driver Frizel and navigator d'Unienville won in their R4L. They were not alone; other Renaults managed very respectable fourth, seventh, eighth, ninth and fourteenth places. More likely victors such as Saab 96s, Mini Coopers and the ultra-tough Peugeots were pushed down the list. The effect on sales and marketing back home was dramatic.

Paris–Dakar Rally

Conceived by Thierry Sabine, the motto of the Paris–Dakar Rally was 'A challenge for those who go. A dream for those who stay behind.' The rally starts in Paris and continues to Algiers before crossing Agadez and ultimately leading to Dakar in Africa. It is extreme in every case: deep sand, scorching heat, relentless sun and freezing temperatures at night. Motorcycles with large, torquey engines and knobbly tyres are the weapon of choice and

The Marreau brothers' Sinpar 4x4 Renault 4 somewhere in the desert. This was the 1980 car in which, despite being up against much more capable all-terrain vehicles and off-road motorcycles, they finished third in general classification. In the previous year's rally, wearing number 131, they finished in fifth place overall but they were the second car behind a Range Rover V8. No ordinary R4, this one had a 130+ bhp R5 Alpine Group 2 engine and was fully proved against sand and water. (Renault)

Never let it be said that R4s can't swim! Another shot of the Marreau brother's 1980 Paris-Dakar rally car in what looks like at least a couple of feet of water. The engine has been rigged for wading with a high-rise exhaust and presumably similar treatment has been applied to the air intake; a sealed ignition system would also be required. It is not reported if the body, chassis and doors were sealed or the brothers wore wetsuits and wellies. (Renault)

won the top three slots in the inaugural 1978 event, with a fourth place Range Rover being the first car across the finishing line.

In 1979 however, brothers Bernard and Claude Marreau drove a 130+ bhp Renault 4 Sinpar – the four-wheel drive version – to fifth place (and the second-placed car), and the following year they managed third in general classification – quite an achievement for a simple utilitarian car, albeit not quite a standard one.

A Rodeo ploughing along a wet and muddy track, Land Rover fashion. Five versions of ACL's plastic mini-SUV were available and each was very grandly named: Evasion (no roof or doors), Chantier (short fabric roof), Coursière (long fabric roof), Quatre Saisons (fabric doors and windows – as pictured here) and Artisanale (commercial type with an opaque roof). Most Rodeos were just front-wheel drive like its donor vehicle but this one has the optional Sinpar 4x4 system. (Renault)

Monte Carlo Rally

As a tribute to the works Renault 4 entries for the 1962 and 1963 Monte Carlo Rallies in which the respective teams of Jo Schlesser and Claude le Guezec, and Jean-Pierre Manzon and Hubert Melot, finished in respectable positions, and also to celebrate the model's then fiftieth anniversary, Renault Classic entered the 2011 Monte Carlo Rally Historique. Three

While Swedes Erik Carlsson and Palm Gunnar were busy up front winning the 1963 Monte Carlo Rally in their Saab 96 Sport, a Renault 4L with Frenchman Jean-Pierre Manzon at the wheel and his co-driving countryman Hubert Melot finished in a very impressive 68th place, and 7th in class. A total of ninety-six cars completed the race and, rather tellingly, 200 retired. This wonderful Alpine shot shows Manzon and Melot in car number 44 winding their way across a snowy *col de montagne* somewhere in the Alps north of Monaco. (Renault)

Another Renault 4L in the Monte Carlo Rally but this time it's the 2011 *Historique* version aimed at classic cars being driven in the spirit of the 1950s and 1960s. To celebrate the golden anniversary of the launch of the car, Renault Classic prepared and entered three R4s. All of them finished with this one, number 4, driven by Jean Ragnotti and co-drivers Sylvain Reisser and Briton Franca Davenport, finishing 169th from a field of 249. (Renault)

cars were prepared for the rigours and challenges of the 1,500-mile route with drivers Manu Guigou, Jean Ragnotti and Michel Leclere, and crews made up from fellow rally people and motoring journalists. All three cars completed the rally without serious mishap in positions 129, 169 and 190 (respectively) out of a total field of 249. One of the cars is now on display in the Renault Classic Collection.

Network Q Rally of Great Britain

Best known by many British rally fans as the Lombard RAC Rally, the sight of a Ford Escort RS1800 being wheeled sideways by Roger Clark around Sutton Park in the Midlands with arch-rival, but good friend, Hannu Mikkola hard on his boot lid is unforgettable. First held in 1932, the event forms a round of the FIA World Rally Championship and, with a new route and now known as the Wales Rally GB, it's the largest of its type in the UK.

It seems rather incongruous now but in 1987 the Renault 4 GTL was homologated and, for just over a decade, GTLs in various liveries popped up in rallies all over the world. In 1998 while (the late) Richard Burns and Robert Reid were heading towards victory in their Mitsubishi, a Renault 4 GTL piloted by António Pinto dos Santos with co-driver Nuno Rodrigues da Silva was spotted towards the back of the field hurtling around the Network Q Rally of Great Britain, receiving more cheers and waves than the rest of the field combined. They finished in a very respectable eighty-second position, eighth in their class, embarrassing neither themselves nor the car.

Pan-American Expedition

According to readers of the French fashion magazine *Elle* the Renault 4 was, in the 1960s, 'the best car for Madame'. That said, twenty-six-year-old Parisian model Michèle Ray decided to put it to the test but rather than a quick spin along the Champs-Élysées, round the Arc de Triomphe and back, she led her three colleagues, Éliane Lucotte, Betty Gérard and Martine Libersart, on a 25,000-mile trip of a lifetime in two standard-issue Renault 4s, from Tierra del Fuego in Chile to Anchorage in Alaska.

Following a four-week training period with Renault where they learnt the basics of keeping a car going when faced with unpaved roads, scorching heat and sub-zero temperatures, on 10 May 1965 the four women in their brace of 4s set off on their mammoth trek. They carried spares, wheels, fuel, water, tools and film equipment but, despite the usually capacious luggage compartment of the cars, they were left with very little space for their clothes and personal items.

Having forded rivers, traversed gorges and mountain passes, including the world's highest at over 15,000 feet where both cars and occupants were short of oxygen, they arrived safely at their destination four months later. They had a multitude of punctures, a broken windscreen and other mishaps but no major mechanical failures. One of the cars has been kept in original condition, just as it finished the marathon, and is part of the Renault Classic Collection.

With a lovely play on words, the four women were referred to as *Les 4 Elle*.

According to French fashion magazine *Elle* it was the Renault 4L that was the 'perfect car for the modern woman' and so, in 1965, Michèle Ray decided to put the theory to the test and led three friends in two 4Ls from Tierra del Fuego on the southern tip of South America right up to Anchorage in Alaska. This photo shows the four women before they set off, and prior to some of the finishing touches having been applied to their cars. (Renault)

The other three women were Éliane Lucotte, Betty Gérard and Martine Libersart, and can be seen here (after sprucing themselves up a little) celebrating completion of the amazing trek. The Renaults look a little battle-scarred but apart from the expected punctures and other annoying snags, they suffered no major problems. The crews admitted that on occasions they broke out their 'charm offensive', usually to help ease their way through the borders and frontiers. Spot the delightful hats made by a keen fan and adorned with model R4s. (Renault)

One of the triumphant cars is now proudly on display as part of the Renault Classic collection in Paris. Some modifications were made including additional lighting and changes to the carburation to help deal with the extremes of altitude encountered on the trip. Notice the bracket on the left-hand front wing to support the cine camera used to record the adventure. (Renault)

Routes du Monde

The 'Routes du Monde' was a project in which Renault would lend young people R4s to travel the world on varying routes giving the participants, all of whom could be no older than twenty-five, a chance to explore the world and at the same time complete some kind of worthwhile project. It started in 1965 and ran for nearly twenty years; in recent times it has effectively been replaced by the 4L Trophy.

The 4L Trophy

The 4L Trophy is an annual humanitarian rally across the Moroccan desert. It was established in 1997 by Jean-Jacques Rey and, with only eighteen to twenty-eight-year-old students allowed to enter and all driving Renault 4s, the overall objective is to deliver nearly 100 tons of school supplies to deprived areas of Africa while also providing each person involved with a deep sense of personal achievement. After driving nearly 4,000 miles through France and Spain from departure points in Bordeaux and Paris, the thousands of participants then cross the mountains and dunes of the Moroccan desert before arriving in Marrakech.

Renault 4L Cross

In 1974, Renault intensified its promotional campaigns by launching the Renault 4L Cross event. Intended to make motor sport accessible to the smaller budget and to identify young talent, only Renault 4s with 845 cc engines were eligible to take part. With low entry fees and a car plus a cash prize for the winner, Michel Duvernay was French champion in 1981. A replica of the winning car was built for the anniversary celebrations and it too now resides in the Renault Classic Collection.

These men trying to coax a recalcitrant bird into a box may think their R4 pick-up is all-French. Vans had been converted into pick-ups by backstreet workshops for years but it was only when Don Raymer of Mechanical Engineering Developments in Somerset, England, saw an opportunity that Renault took notice and decided to supply them officially. MED supplied the first prototype in 1974, registered its design and won a contract with Renault to convert F4 and F6 vans into pick-ups for the UK market. Renault later turned to Teilhol (formerly ACL, producers of the Rodeo) and offered both left- and right-hand drive versions. (Renault)

A marketing shot showing the usefulness of the Renault 4 van, especially with the so-called giraffe hatch opened. This one also has very serious-looking mudflaps and the wind-down spare wheel carrier beneath the rear of the vehicle (similarly situated on the saloons) can also just be seen. (Renault)

Another Renault 4 in everyday use and wearing its battle damage well. With a roof rack to extend its luggage-carrying capability, this one also sports a tow bar. This was spotted languishing in a little street off the main road in Manacor, the second largest town on the island of Mallorca, part of the Spanish Balearic Islands. (Smith)

Renault 4 vans were useful the world over. It looks like the delivery driver is very happy to hand over a package to the recipient high in some mountain retreat. This is the version with the optional opening side windows. Maybe he's a family man, self-employed possibly, and this vehicle also serves as his weekend transport? (Renault)

A very early (mid-1961) R4 at rest. The owner might be sitting with their family on their patio overlooking a sunlit valley in southern France about to enjoy a generous bowl of cassoulet, a baguette and a glass or two of red. (Peyre)

With the need to post this very appropriate advert for the very vehicle he has travelled in, this chap has made full use of the 'giraffe' slot at the top of the rear door opening. Given the bumper shape and treatment, this F4 is quite an early one. Health and safety precautions are not much in evidence here. (Renault)

6

Legacy

Now practically three decades on from when production ceased, the Renault 4 remains on the automotive landscape. Many remain in regular use, not so many in Britain where corrosion has rendered them virtually extinct, but in parts of Europe, Asia, Africa and South America where they are still a fairly regular sight. Enthusiasts of the R4 – 'Trelleurs'

This couple may be happy with their ribbed bonnet R4 fitted with snazzy bumpers and tripod hubcaps but maybe their stolen weekend away from the office has now come to an end. From the state of the car's tyres, it looks like they've been exercising the long-travel suspension with a little off-roading, but nevertheless they've found a lovely spot to enjoy the setting sun. (Renault)

as they are known – have ensured that, with help from various clubs and publications dedicated to the model, surviving vehicles are restored, modified, rallied or simply used on a daily basis. They are doing exactly what they were designed to do: carrying people and goods over the roads and tracks of the world. Throughout its life this car has been acceptable for everyone; it transcends and blurs the lines of age and social groups, and has adapted effortlessly to all lands and all cultures.

A total of 8,126,000 Renault 4s (although the factory estimate of 8,135,424 is often quoted) were built or assembled in twenty-eight countries, and sold in more than 100. Even more remarkably, production and sales covered six continents with only Antarctica missing out – and more than half of the total sales were outside France. Nearer to home, thousands of Renaults – including the 4 – rolled out of the plant in Wexford, Ireland, and the Renault 4 was now not only the top French *voiture* but the world's third best-selling car, and as such it has become a truly global one.

Despite being comprehensively outsold at home and abroad, the Citroën 2CV has undoubtedly been taken to the heart of the French nation and is considered by many to epitomise Gallic motoring charm. The Renault 4 however deserves a similar level of reverence but perhaps it has simply been too capable and ubiquitous, just blending into the background and steadily dwindling in numbers before being spotted for what it actually is. After sixty years in the making, it's the Renault 4 that should be considered to be the *real* French people's car.

Vive la Quatrelle!